GW00455517

THE WORLD,
THE FLESH
AND THE DEVIL

THE WORLD, THE FLESH AND THE DEVIL

JACK HAY

JOHN RITCHIE LTD
CHRISTIAN PUBLICATIONS

40 Beansburn, Kilmarnock, Scotland

ISBN-13: 978 1 912522 32 3

Typeset by Pete Barnsley (Creativehoot.com)

Printed by Bell & Bain Ltd., Glasgow

"Mine enemies are lively, and they are strong…Forsake me not, O Lord…Make haste to help me, O Lord my salvation."

Psalm 38.19-22

CONTENTS

FOREWORD

The title of this book is, of course, not original!

The expression: *"The World, The Flesh and the Devil"* can be found in Christian writings that date back many, many centuries.

For example, *'The Book of Common Prayer'*, which first appeared in 1549, encouraged Christians to pray:

"From all the deceits of the world, the flesh, and the devil, Good Lord, deliver us".

In 1678, John Bunyan published his *'Pilgrim's Progress'*. Part III of the book is described as showing: *"the several Dangers and Difficulties he met with in his Journey; and the many Victories he obtained over the World, the Flesh and the Devil; together with his happy Arrival at the Celestial City"*.

A nation can face attack in three spheres - on land, at sea and in the air. A Christian was said to face attack from these three sources – The World, the Flesh and the Devil.

Christian life was seen as a strenuous struggle. There were foes to face. There were defeats to avoid. There were victories to win. This was regarded as a continual conflict. Not limited, but rather lifelong.

In recent years, however, another view has emerged. As A W Tozer put it:

"People think of the world, not as a battleground, but as a playground. We are not here to fight; we are here to frolic. We are not in a foreign land; we are at home."

The world was no longer viewed as a foe, but as a friend. The threat posed by the flesh and even by the Devil was likewise minimised.

Such a perception is disastrous!

In this very useful little book, Jack Hay takes us back to the Scriptures.

He shows us that in the New Testament, these three foes are described. He also shows us that at various points in the Old Testament, these same foes are depicted.

This is indeed a battleground!

Jack says towards the end of Chapter 1, "'Know your enemy' is sound advice". Indeed it is! It has rightly been called: "The first rule of war!" Methodically and meticulously, he deals with our enemies.

But, this is no dry academic work. What you will read here is immensely practical. Jack shows that if we want to make progress in our spiritual lives, if we want to please God, we will need to fight! Very useful guidance is shared in that respect. At times, Jack is very blunt – explicit examples of areas of danger are specified - but this is always intended to be for our benefit and blessing.

In July 2017, Jack gave ministry on this subject over a weekend in Deri, Wales. Those who were present found the teaching very informative and very challenging. The suggestion was subsequently made to Jack that what he had said should be made available to a wider audience. He agreed to write on the subject – and I am glad he has done so. I have been helped by reading this book. No matter where you are in the Christian life, you will find it helpful too.

Jack Hay is a powerful Gospel preacher and gifted Bible teacher. He is also the author of a number of publications. This latest one is to be welcomed.

It has been my privilege on countless occasions to listen to him. It has been my privilege on three occasions to preach with him. It is now my privilege to write this Foreword for him.

I warmly commend this book to you.

Fraser A Munro
Windygates, Fife
April 2018

CHAPTER 1

THREE
FORMIDABLE FOES

Conflict! The historical books of the Old Testament are full of it. In Genesis ch.4 there is the record of the first murder, and the first battles and wars feature as early as chapter 14. As the history of Israel develops there is a steady stream of palace intrigues, assassinations and military coups as well as continual confrontations with foreign foes. Bloodshed and strife are never far from the surface.

In particular, the book of Judges mentions a whole range of nations who attacked and subdued Israel at various stages, and that hostility extended into the days of the monarchy. Israel's conflicts illustrate the spiritual warfare experienced by believers of this present era. The New Testament constantly employs military metaphors in connection with Christian living. For example, there are a number of references to armour (e.g. Eph 6.10-20), and Timothy was encouraged to be "a good soldier of Jesus

Christ" (2 Tim 2.3). War, hand-to-hand conflict, boxing and wrestling are all in the mix; Christians are seen as combatants. The Christian life is not for softies for our enemies are as numerous as Israel's; there is the constant need to be as skilful as a strategist, as lively as a lookout, and as courageous as a commando.

Caleb's Three Enemies

Caleb was a notable warrior, and among multiple enemies, he had three in his sights. They were three giants, the sons of Anak, and they were obstacles to his ambition to have Hebron as his inheritance; he expelled them effectively to possess their city (Josh 15.14). The meaning of the word "Hebron" provides an illustration of our need to live in *fellowship* with God. To enjoy Hebron, the three enemies had to be overpowered; similarly, among all the enemies arrayed against the believer, there are three major foes who must be resisted if we are to please God; our three chief enemies are The World, The Flesh and The Devil.

Benaiah's Three Enemies

Benaiah was one of David's mighty men and he too had to face a trio of foes (2 Sam 23.20-23). In reviewing Benaiah's career, David highlighted three notable events in his life, three memorable victories when these adversaries were overcome. The first victory was over two "lionlike men of Moab". The second was when he "slew a lion in the midst of a pit in time of snow". The third was when "he slew an Egyptian, a goodly man". The origins of Moab make him a picture of The Flesh, the devil is likened to a lion (1 Pet 5.8), and Egypt is an illustration of The World. So Benaiah's exploits picture the believer's conflict with The World, The Flesh and The Devil.

Pre-Conversion; The Dominance of the Three Enemies

Paul explained to the Ephesians that before our conversion, these three enemies dominated us, and he grouped them like the three sons of Anak or the three protagonists of Benaiah. (Eph 2.1-3). "Ye walked according to the course of this **world**", just drifting with the crowd, adopting the world's standards, participating in its pleasures and conforming to its fashions. "**The prince of the power of the air**" dictated our attitude and the devil is seen as the one who promotes a spirit of insubordination in every human heart. We lived "in the **lusts of our flesh**, fulfilling the desires of the flesh and of the mind". Sinful desires were unfettered, and bodily urges and intellectual fantasies were indulged. It makes dismal reading, but thankfully with verse 4 there comes the welcome, "But God", and as a result of His intervention and the experience of salvation (v.5) the whole picture changed; we have been freed from the tyranny of the world, the flesh and the devil.

Post-Conversion; Warnings of Their Continued Activity

However, these former slave masters feel cheated, extremely irritated that we were rescued by the Lord Jesus, and so we have become the targets for malicious attacks as they do all in their power to annul our effectiveness for God. As stated, in Ephesians 2 Paul groups them in relation to our unconverted days, but John brackets them when warning believers (1 Jn 2.14-17). Those to whom he wrote had progressed in their Christian lives, and in spiritual conflict had "overcome the wicked one", but we do know that "**the wicked one**" will not lie down! We learn from his attack on the Lord Jesus that he can withdraw defeated "for a season" (Lk 4.13), with the inference that he will regroup and mount further offensives. So John's readers could never afford to be complacent, and to add to their danger, the other enemies were lurking nearby. Thus John says, "Love not **the world**", and in referring to "the lust of **the flesh**" he shows that the flesh is an internal traitor, which co-operates with the world and its prince to destroy our enjoyment of the things of God and to dilute our commitment to the work of God. Thus John brings together, the world and the flesh and the devil; two of these are external foes and the other is the conspirator within us.

Sometimes it is impossible to detect which enemy we are facing, and to be frank, at times it can be all three together just as Moab, Amalek and Ammon were allies in attacking Israel (Judg 3.13). However, in this study we will examine each of them individually to gather some Bible teaching about the origins, features, and activities of all three. "Know your enemy" is sound advice, and it is hoped that if we familiarise ourselves with the character and tactics of our enemies, we will be better equipped to repel their onslaughts, and that our lives will become impregnable citadels against both their frontal attacks and their subtle ambushes.

CHAPTER 2

THE WORLD: THE PLANET, THE AGE, AND THE SYSTEM

New Testament Words for "World".

At this point, be patient as we highlight one or two technicalities before moving into our theme! In the New Testament, there are three main words translated "world" and these are as follows.

- There is the word that means "the inhabited earth" (*Strong's Concordance* 3625). According to Online Bible statistics, it is used 15 times, and to give some samples, Caesar Augustus decreed that "all *the world* should be taxed" (Lk 2.1). In the future, the Gospel of the kingdom "shall be preached in all *the world*" (Mt 24.14). The citizens of Thessalonica claimed that the preachers had "turned *the world* upside down" (Acts

17.6). The Lord Jesus used the word when predicting the culmination of the Great Tribulation, speaking of "those things which are coming on *the earth*" (Lk 21.26), the only occasion when the KJV uses the word "earth" to translate the word. Generally then, this word means the earth and on occasions by extension, the inhabitants of the earth.

- The second word is used extensively, with a variety of translations depending on context (*Strong* 165). Generally it carries the idea of an age of time and it is translated "world" in Scriptures like Galatians 1.4, where we are told that we have been delivered "from this present evil *world*", or 2 Corinthians 4.4 where the devil is described as "the god of this *world*", or Romans 12.2 where we forbidden to be "conformed to this *world*". Often, the word is used as a figure of speech for the moral and spiritual conditions obtaining in the world during the age being described.

- The third word for world is the one that will feature most in our references to the believer's enemies. It is the Greek word *kosmos* (*Strong* 2889). I mention the Greek word because it is one that preachers occasionally use without any explanation, expecting everyone to know exactly what they mean! English dictionaries explain that it is the Greek word from which we get our English word "cosmetic" because the word carries the idea of something that is nicely arranged. In fact, on the only occasion in the KJV where the word is not translated "world" the rendering is "adorning"; "Whose adorning let it not be that outward adorning of plaiting the hair, and of wearing of gold, or of putting on of apparel" (1 Pet 3.3).

The meaning of *kosmos* is determined by context, with three main connotations.

- Sometimes it means the world as a planet, what we call planet earth; for example, when Paul was preaching at Athens, he spoke of "God that made the world and all things therein" (Acts 17.24).

- Sometimes it means mankind, the people of the world. John 3.16 is very familiar in this connection, "For God so loved the world...".

- Relevant to our subject is the third aspect of the word; sometimes it means "the present condition of human affairs, in alienation from and opposition to God" (W.E. Vine). This world system has developed under the patronage of Satan, for "the whole world lieth in the wicked one" (1 Jn 5.19 most translations). He is the mastermind behind the system and the one who dictates its attitudes, trends and fashions, for he is "the prince of this world" (Jn 12.31; 14.30; 16.11).

The Lord Jesus in His prayer in John 17 brings these three aspects of *kosmos* together. Believers have not been taken "out of the world" (v.15), that is, they have not been removed from the planet. "They are not of the world" (v.16), that is, they do not take character from the world system; they are not part of it. They have been "sent...into the world" (v.18), that is, the Lord has sent us among men with the message of the gospel.

"This World's Goods"

Sometimes we speak of the world in abstract terms, but it has tangible manifestations such as its "goods" (1 Jn 3.17), that is, our material possessions. In themselves they are not evil, but the Lord warned about being so preoccupied with them that it amounts trying to "gain the whole world". In so doing we lose our lives, losing our lives in the sense of squandering time, energy and resources that could have been used profitably for God if we just diligently pursued the path of discipleship (Mt 16.26). Nothing can compensate for the tragedy of a wasted life. Avoid grasping greedily for this world's goods. Accumulating gadgets, itching for bigger and better things, cluttering our lives with the trappings of recreation and hankering for constant exotic breaks from the routine of life are all part the world's mind-set, and it all requires an abundance of "this world's goods". In many cases these dreams can only become concrete reality by pruning spiritual commitments and allowing Christian service to become the equivalent of a spectator sport. What world are you living for?

"The Spirit of the World".

The Bible also speaks of the invisible attitudes and influences of the world, the "spirit of the world" (1 Cor 2.12), "the wisdom of this world" (ch.3.19), and "the fashion of this world" (ch.7.31). Paul augments this by speaking to Titus about "worldly lusts" (Tit 2.12), and Peter shows that these lusts are corrupting and polluting (2 Pet 1.4; 2.20). Notice the development revealed in these quotations. What starts as an attitude of mind becomes the perceived wisdom of the day because it excludes God and His inhibiting standards. It then becomes a lifestyle that corrupts and pollutes. We are left with the impression that the world system is an abomination to God, an affront to His holiness, and an audacious challenge to His sovereign authority in the universe. It is wonderful that we are among those who have "escaped the corruption that is in the world through lust" (2 Pet 1.4), but we must consistently "keep (ourselves) unspotted from the world" (James 1.27).

"The Men of the World".

The men who express these attitudes themselves come under the umbrella term, "the world", so in reading of the world we are sometimes confronted not only with the organisation that has Satan as its prince, but with the people who are caught up in the organisation and who happily regard themselves as "men of the world" (Ps 17.14). They are blatantly indifferent to God; "the world by wisdom knew not God" (1 Cor 1.21). They hate the Son of God; "the world...hated me before it hated you" (Jn 15.18). They have no perception of the Spirit of God; "the world...seeth him not, neither knoweth him" (Jn 14.17). Their general aversion to deity is extended to God's people; "Marvel not, my brethren, if the world hate you" (1 Jn 3.13). Incited by the devil, their natural antagonism towards the triune God is vented against believers. Thus holiness is ridiculed and piety is pilloried. Right up to this present time, many believers worldwide have experienced beatings, torture, imprisonment and even martyrdom because of their loyalty to Christ. The chill winds of persecution still blow across the planet as the world expresses its hatred of anything or anyone connected to God. Thus the term "the world" is not just a vague concept; it embraces solid possessions, expresses attitudes, and encompasses men and women, the flesh and blood exponents of "all that is in the world" (1 Jn 2.16).

CHAPTER 3

THE ORIGINS
OF THE WORLD

We have seen already that our three enemies conspire together to oppose us, and in particular, there is an obvious bond between the world and its prince, Satan himself. Having deluded Eve and effected The Fall (Gen 3), his next plan was to get the world system up and running and he found a willing accomplice in the first man ever to be born. Cain is described as being "of that wicked one" (1 Jn 3.12), and the building blocks of the world system were put in place by Cain and his descendants as recorded in Genesis 4. They did everything in their power to make life without God at least tolerable. It is true that that whole line of humanity was wiped out at the flood so there is no one in the world descended from Cain, but the world system was revived after the flood, and in particular Nimrod defied God (Gen 10.8-10) and was undoubtedly a main mover in the events surrounding the Babel incident of chapter 11 where man's arrogance and rebellion were frustrated by God confounding human language.

But to go back to Cain and his descendants; what we are told about them throws up different features of the world that were introduced in these ancient times, characteristics that are still in place today, and any one of them could prove to be a snare for the believer in Christ.

Counterfeit Worldly Religion

No sooner had Adam sinned than he was overcome by a deep sense of shame. Fig leaves were no answer to his humiliation and God Himself had to clothe our first parents with coats of skin (Gen 3.21). Implicit in the statement is the slaughter of a victim. Fleecing a sheep would have clad the guilty pair, but from day one of the history of fallen man, God was showing that acceptance with Him must be on the basis of sacrifice. That information must have been communicated to the family, because Abel "brought of the firstlings of his flock" and "the Lord had respect unto Abel and to his offering" (ch.4.4). Cain had other ideas and "brought of the fruit of the ground an offering unto the Lord" (v.3). Essentially, this was a bloodless offering and undoubtedly it had taken time to produce. In the previous chapter the ground had been cursed and it would have taken considerable effort to encourage that cursed ground to yield something beautiful and tasty. There had also been the promise of thorns and thistles so Cain would have known the frustration of the never-ending battle with the weeds. Further, God had given notice that human nourishment would be available at the expense of sweat-inducing toil so Cain had perspired profusely in producing his offering. Time, labour, and sweat; to arrange this gift there was a tremendous input of each, and yet it was valueless and Cain was rejected.

In Cain's activity we see the prototype of worldly religion, the rejection of God's plan in favour of man's ideas. It seems so logical to the human mind that effort will please God, and that it is so needless to take life and shed blood when our salvation lies in our own hands! Every world religion is works driven, whether it be the great eastern religions or mysticism or so-called Christianity. Sadly much of what is labelled "Christian" embraces systems that are ritualistically orientated, and they reject the plan of salvation that issues from God's grace, a salvation that is based on the work of Christ at the cross and which benefits people on the principle of faith alone. Faith has been substituted by self-help, self-effort and self-improvement demands. It all started with Cain who "was of that wicked one" the devil himself, who has consistently "blinded the minds of them which believe not" (2 Cor 4.4).

Many of these blinded souls are far from being atheistic and judge themselves to be devout and respectable, but they have "gone in the way of Cain" (Jude 11); they have never learned that salvation is "not of works, lest any man should boast" (Eph 2.9). So the devil still uses religion to keep large swathes of humanity on the road to hell; worldly religion is still alive and well and genuine believers should steer clear of involvement with it. Avoid mimicking its hierarchical structure, its so-called worship style and the gimmicks it employs to catch and hold its devotees.

Sometimes believers are astounded at the seemingly spectacular success of some of the cults, many of them claiming to be the fastest growing religion in the world. Their growth rate should not surprise us. John says of the exponents of false religion, "They are of the world: therefore speak they of the world, and the world heareth them" (1 Jn 4.5). In other words, they are peddling the different brands of worldly religion that hold a charm for worldly people and so they embrace it. The devil is happy enough to transfer his captives from any form of perversion or addiction to religious respectability provided it does not involve the life-changing soul-saving experience of conversion to Christ.

Violence

Cain's rejection annoyed him greatly; his rage spilled over into violence and soon his brother lay dead in the field (Gen 4.8), so for the very first time a man had died. It was not too long before Cain's descendant Lamech was guilty of another homicide (v.23), so violence was becoming engrained in the world system and by the days of Noah "the earth was filled with violence" (Gen 6.11). After the flood, the violence continued throughout the book of Genesis. There is the first mention of war (Gen 14.2); sexual violence flares at Sodom (ch.19.4-11); sibling rivalry almost leads to fratricide (ch.27.41). Going into the book of Exodus, the ruling classes use threats and affliction to keep the workers enslaved (Ex 1-11), and so the sad liturgy of aggression proceeds, for the world's prince was "a murderer from the beginning" (Jn 8.44), and his ambition is to keep the world in a constant state of commotion and fear and it will be thus until the Lord Jesus introduces an administration in which peace will pervade the planet for one thousand years (Is 2.2-4).

In the meantime, international tension, domestic violence, sexual harassment, and workplace conflict are all the order of the day. The "entertainment" industry capitalises on the public's insatiable appetite for the portrayal of extreme behaviour, and what is projected on screens is saturated with loud threatening language and scenes of inhuman physical violence. What is fictional soon becomes fact as some of the minds that are exposed to such horrors dare to replicate them in real life. This is another feature of the world that should be a no-go area for the believer. In his epistle, John stresses that even an aggressive attitude is out of place for someone professing to be in the family of God. "Whosoever hateth his brother is a murderer: and ye know that no murderer hath eternal life abiding in him" (1 Jn 3.15). John argues that a belligerent "brother" is probably not a brother at all!

City Life

Cain "builded a city" (Gen 4.17), and his actions constitute another of his acts of defiance. God had decreed that he would be "a wanderer" (v.12 RV), and in building a city he seemed to be declaring his intention to outmanoeuvre God by staying put in the one location. It appears to be an attempt to achieve solidarity on the part of those opposed to God by binding them as a unit, and that sense of camaraderie is captured in the vast number of clubs, societies, associations and guilds that have proliferated throughout the world. Common interests cement people, but the net effect is to distract them from the things that matter most, salvation and the need for a right relationship with God. David said, "I have hated the congregation of evil doers; and will not sit with the wicked" (Ps 26.5). He was saying that he avoided the places where the ungodly congregate to pursue their worldly activities. In modern times, such gathering centres include public houses, sports arenas, theatres and the like. Often, the behaviour, language and attitudes exhibited at such venues are less than wholesome and can be virulently infectious. When Peter sat with the enemies of his Lord, it did not take long for him to be using the same kind of language, as he laced his conversation with oaths and curses.

> *Can I take part with those*
> *Who nailed Him to the tree?*
> *And where His name is never praised*
> *Is there the place for me?*
> *Nay, world! I turn away,*
> *Though thou seem fair and good.*
> *That friendly outstretched hand of thine*
> *Is stained with Jesus' blood.*
> (Margaret Mauro)

The name of Cain's city is significant; he called it after his son Enoch, and the name means "dedicated". God had a dedicated man who walked with Him (ch.5.22), but the world has its dedicated men too, dedicated to whatever aspect of the world that has charmed them. Pre-conversion, Paul and Titus had been among the world's dedicated men, "serving (as slaves) divers lusts and pleasures" (Tit 3.3).

Some find their pleasure in the realm of sport and their dedication affects every area of their lives. They operate a strict diet when their friends are gorging themselves. They are pounding the roads when their friends are still in bed. They are in the gym when their friends are socialising; dedicated. For some the role is that of a spectator, but the team is their god and the stadium their cathedral; dedicated. Others are entertainment enthusiasts and their heroes are the stars of stage and screen. Their commitment is expressed in the distances travelled and the expenditure involved in attending live performances, and all the paraphernalia connected with their idols are must-have items; dedicated. It would be wonderful if believers were to express similar dedication to the things of God and like loyal Enoch, to walk with God.

Moral Deviation

Cain's descendant Lamech created another precedent that became embedded in the world system when for the first time there was a departure from the God-given pattern for marriage, a one man/one woman relationship; "Lamech took unto him two wives" (Gen 4.19). Before long in the book of Genesis, the Scriptural pattern for marriage was being compromised in different ways, and trends were set in motion, which continue to run until this present day. At Sodom, homosexuality became the order of the day (Gen 19). In the same chapter incest reared its head. Dinah was living with Prince Shechem without being married to him (ch.34). Prostitution features in ch.38 and seduction in ch.39. It did not take long for sexual deviation to take hold and become an integral part of the world system, so from ancient times there has been a revolt against the divine ideal for marriage. It has created immense misery on the part of those who have been cheated, and in many many cases it has caused huge physical and psychological damage to the perpetrators (Rom 1.24-27). Scripture warns that God judges fornicators and adulterers (Heb 13.4).

As far as the Western World is concerned, promiscuity mushroomed in the 1960s and has reached tidal-wave proportions. What now passes as acceptable comedy would formerly have been regarded as totally offensive. Films and T.V. serials depict illicit relationships as normal, for sadly, the fact is that what is being portrayed has become the order of the day although abnormal from a Biblical standpoint. One of the features of the "last days" is that men shall be "unholy", and it is being acted out in society today (2 Tim 3.1-2). Generally, people are preoccupied with "sex" and it receives massive press coverage and occupies a large proportion of general conversation. Preoccupation with it is endemic to the world system but as the children of God we are called upon to "cleanse ourselves from all filthiness of the flesh and spirit, perfecting holiness in the fear of God" (2 Cor 7.1).

Agriculture and Industry

Lamech's son Jabal pioneered rural life as opposed to city life. He was "the father of such as dwell in tents, and of such as have cattle" (Gen 4.20). His half-brother Tubal-cain spearheaded industrial activity as he researched and lectured on matters relating to "brass and iron" (v.22). Agriculture and industry are the two great pillars of the world's economy, depicted in the hammer and sickle of communism. The farm and the factory are the world's great employers; the mass of its workforce participates in one or other of these activities; they are fundamental to the wellbeing of earth's population.

Believers are unavoidably involved, either as part of the workforce or in management. It is a Biblical principle that "if any will not work, neither let him eat" (2 Thess 3.10 R.V.). To be a wage earner and a breadwinner for the family is a duty endorsed by Scripture, even although it entails an involvement with part of the world system. Paul speaks about this in 1 Corinthians ch.7, and we are told to "use this world, as not abusing it" (v.31), that is, not using it to the full. We must avoid getting sucked into a state of total commitment to its ways and demands. The job should never dominate, for "the time is short" (v.29). Paul's argument is that our time here is too limited to allow domestic issues with their celebrations and sorrows to take us over. Neither should business and employment with their stresses and demands impinge on spiritual responsibilities.

Believers need help from God to discern where to draw the line when it comes to "using the world". The thinking of the world has infected the educational system that prepares people for employment, and in the day-to-day routine of work, many of the Lord's people are faced with problems of conscience over ethical questions and matters of honesty that would present no difficulty to worldly colleagues. It takes courage to take a Biblical stand on many of these issues.

Music

Lamech's son Jubal broke new ground as far as musical instruments were concerned; "he was the father of all such as handle the harp and pipe", and thus humanity was introduced to both stringed and wind instruments (Gen 4.21 most translations). In many spheres, the world knows the value of the emotional effects of music. In the entertainment industry it is a multi-billion pound money-spinner. Each genre has its own followers with their personal preferences and the cash to spend in the pursuit of their pleasure. The world of popular music has evolved from the emotional ballads that portrayed the heartbreak of a jilted boyfriend to raucous incitements to immorality, drug abuse and rebellion. Young believers need to be extremely guarded about what passes through their ear buds; it could be so polluting.

Every nation has its anthem to stir loyalty, and their citizens experience tingling sensations of patriotism when the first notes are struck! Regimental bands are no mere addendums to military life; the music is calculated to stir and embolden the warriors (2 Chr 20.21-22). Protest and freedom movements have capitalised on the emotive effects of the music, a notable example being Bob Dylan's *"Blowing in the Wind"*. Religion has also tapped into this valuable medium with instruments and choirs being major features of the regular "services" to stir the spirit of "worship". Nebuchadnezzar understood its worth when he combined stern threats with the moving effects of an orchestra with its six specific instruments "and all kinds of music" (Dan 3.5).

As far as believers are concerned, singing is a legitimate expression of joy (James 5.13) and one of the consequences of being filled with the Spirit (Eph 5.18-19). In the Old Testament instrumental music and choral arrangements played a massive part in temple worship but these features were never carried into the Christian era. All the externals such as the sights and sounds and smells connected with Judaism were terminated with the introduction of the new order of things. Worship today is not induced by these appeals to human senses, but rather by the activity of the Holy Spirit. "We are the circumcision, who worship by the Spirit of God, and glory in Christ Jesus, and have no confidence in the flesh" (Phil 3.3 R.V.). True expressions of worship are those prompted by Him. In New Testament times believers were encouraged and motivated by the teaching of the Word of God without anything resembling the "Christian musical entertainment" that occupies such a large place in evangelical circles today.

Poetry

The first recorded attempts at poetry came from Lamech with the narration of a killing, a revenge attack on someone who had assaulted him (Gen 4.23-24). For the first time mankind was trying to avoid a dull prosaic way of presenting facts by setting them out all wrapped up in fine language and with words that almost dance. The cultural side of the world was now up and running. It is true that many poems are harmless and do much to excite interest in things that are pleasant to observe, but it does seem that this first poem set a bad precedent that has been perpetuated; it glorifies immorality and violence.

The poem was addressed to his two wives and we have already noted that that situation was a violation of God's original intention for a one-man one-woman relationship. It condones violent conduct and encourages the spirit of vengeance as well as being an expression of self-vindication. The cultural side of the world can be a platform for self-expression that proves to be influential, and philosophies expressed in charming language can be so harmful because they are bereft of any input from heaven. "The pen is mightier than the sword" is an old adage, and the power of the pen has been well-utilised in the world system to influence minds and to chart courses that are in complete disharmony with the Word of God.

CHAPTER 4

THE BELIEVER
AND THE WORLD

The Lord's Teaching

New Testament writers frequently refer to the relationship that believers have with the world and the attitude that they should adopt towards it. In every case, the teaching is negative, for nothing positive could ever come from any interaction with a system that is so blatantly opposed to the Christian's Saviour. As cited already, in His prayer the Lord Jesus said that we are "not of the world" (Jn 17.14-16). We do not take character from the world, but rather, we have the same status as the Lord Himself, "not of the world, even as I am not of the world". His links are with heaven and so too are ours (Jn 8.23). Thus the world's values, standards and interests are foreign to us. When we were part of the world, these things absorbed us, but the Father has given us to the Lord Jesus "out of the world" (Jn 17.6).

Our transfer from the one sphere to the other was at great cost, for the Saviour "gave himself for our sins, that he might deliver us from this present evil world (age)" (Gal 1.4). The sacrificial work of the Lord Jesus has not only dealt with "our sins", but was necessary to liberate us from the hold that the world with all its evil had upon us. That is why it must be so grieving to the Lord to see any of us allowing ourselves to be ensnared by worldly interests or adopting a worldly outlook.

The same Epistle to the Galatians explains that our association with Christ in His crucifixion has terminated our links with the world. "God forbid that I should glory, save in the cross of our Lord Jesus Christ, by whom the world is crucified unto me, and I unto the world" (ch.6.14). In the context, Paul is probably majoring on the religious world, but it is a general principle, that because of the cross, we are permanently finished for this world in its various facets, and it is likewise over for us. How is that concept working out practically in your life? Are we in practice demonstrating the Lord's assertion that we are "not of the world"? Isaac Watts' hymn *"When I survey the wondrous cross"* is sung regularly. Most hymnbooks omit the following relevant verse.

His dying crimson, like a robe,
Spread o'er His body on the tree:
Then I am dead to all the globe,
And all the globe is dead to me.

James

How is "pure religion" displayed before God? According to James, among other things it means "to keep... unspotted from the world" (James 1.27). We have noted already that there is "corruption ... in the world through lust" (2 Pet 1.4), and minds and manners can be sullied by contact with it. Hence the need for endless caution in avoiding anything that could have that defiling effect. It means that every activity has to be well monitored; every well that spews out vulgar licentious material must be capped. In practical terms that necessitates stringently regulating reading material whether it be newspapers, magazines or novels. It involves the merciless curtailment of what is viewed either on a large screen in the living room or privately via the cell phone, tablet or laptop. It entails filtering everything to which we listen. That is all involved in remaining "unspotted from the world". Remember, James says that it is "before our God and Father" (R.V.); your Father is the silent interested observer of all that interests you and it grieves Him when there is any contaminating activity.

James comes back to the subject of the world in chapter 4; "Ye adulteresses, know ye not that the friendship of the world is enmity with God?" (v.4 most translations). He is expressing two dramatic facts. First, the believer who befriends the world is like a woman who has betrayed her marriage vow, an adulteress. Second, to befriend the world is to take up a hostile stance towards God, to become His enemy (v.4). Just to clear up a point; James is not encouraging a cold, aloof attitude to the people around us. An unfriendly disposition will counteract attempts to interest them in the gospel. What is entailed in friendship with the world is to be involved with people to the extent that your leisure time is spent in their company pursuing the same pleasures and frequenting the same haunts. The company that we keep is crucial to our own spiritual state and development. "I am a companion of all them that fear thee, and of them that keep thy precepts" (Ps 119.63). "I have not sat with vain persons...I have hated the congregation of evil doers" (Ps 26.4-5). "Evil company doth corrupt good manners" (1 Cor 15.33 R.V.). The same epistle by James that raises the possibility of us being friends of the world speaks about Abraham who was "the Friend of God" (ch.2.23). We really have to decide whose friendship we want!

An adulteress; the metaphor was used frequently in the Old Testament when Israel had a dalliance with idols; now it is applied to the believer who gets too close to the world. For them, the Scripture has spoken in vain (v.5); that is, the whole tenor of the Word of God that warns against the dangers of involvement with the world has been ignored. Further, they have not taken into account that God is never satisfied with divided affections; "the Lord thy God (is) a jealous God" (Ex 20.5) as implied in the second question of James 4.5 in most translations. Let us all be careful to avoid the kind of contact with the world that renders us disloyal to God and even openly hostile to Him.

Paul

Paul's negative teaching about the world is to tell us, "And be not conformed to this world" (Rom 12.2). It has often been observed that if we get verse 1 in place by presenting our bodies a living sacrifice, then there will be no danger of us being conformed to the world. Commitment to God and devotion to Christ, consecration to the service of God and sacrificial Christian living will all be powerful positive antidotes to conformity to the world. We all do well to ask ourselves if there has ever been that moment of surrender.

The word "conformed" is used by Peter when he says, "as obedient children, not *fashioning yourselves* (same Greek word) according to the former lusts in your ignorance" (1 Pet 1.14). There the appeal is to avoid allowing our Christian lives to become a moulded replica of what we were before conversion. The change has to be stark and obvious. In Romans 12.2 the appeal is to avoid becoming a moulded replica of what is normal in the culture and lifestyle of the age around us. Styles, attitudes, pastimes and ambitions all reflect the anti-God feeling that is generated by "the god of this age", Satan himself. The world has no time for non-conformists and the danger is that we bow to peer pressure. It expects everyone to toe the line, and to be perceptibly different demands courage, for we all naturally prefer recognition to ridicule. Being distinct in morals, ethics, interests and the general round of life can mean being ostracised by fellow-students, colleagues, neighbours or relatives. It can be a lonely existence and hence the need for the support mechanism of the assembly to be in place, the society of the saints providing a veritable haven for those who are charting the stormy waters of being misunderstood and cold-shouldered.

John

If the Lord tells us that we are not of the world, and James commands us to be unspotted from the world, and Paul says we must not be conformed to the world, John insists that we must not love the world; "Love not the world" (1 Jn 2.15). While this is applicable to us all, in the context it was addressed to those described as "young men", those who had advanced from spiritual infancy and whose growth was evidenced in that they were strong.

Spiritual strength, love for the Scriptures and victory over the devil all told the story that these believers had taken strides of progress in their Christian lives. But John anticipated that even people like that could be allured and sidetracked by the world. The lesson is that no one is safe.

"Love not the world". Family members cannot love both their Father and the world at the same time (v.15). God is never satisfied with divided affections; He demands the unswerving loyalty that is His due. The Father and the world are incompatible.

Nothing connected with "the world" takes character from the Father (v.16), and John specifies three features of the world system that can cripple the believer. As in verse 14, items one and three seem to revolve around item two. The lust of the eyes stokes the lust of the flesh and the lust of the eyes incites the desire for ostentatious living, "the ostentation of the life" (YLT). It was "the lust of the eyes" that prompted the "lust of the flesh" in Samson; He "**saw** a woman". He "**saw** there an harlot", (Judg 14.1; 16.1). It was "the lust of the eyes" that ensnared David. "He **saw** a woman", (2 Sam 11.2). In an age in which visual images play an enormous part in entertainment, the attitude of Job is apt; "I made a covenant with mine eyes" (Job 31.1). In His teaching, the Lord Jesus linked looking and lusting (Mt 5.28); we stress again then the need to avoid suggestive and provocative reading material, videos, or internet sites.

Advertisers know the value of promoting their products through the eye, and their "must-have" items are presented in a flashy way, which appeals to the "pride of life". What we see we covet, not because it is a necessity, but because we are pretentious, and our showy possessions give an illusionary sense of smug contentment! John sees it as worldliness.

His subsequent statement should shatter these illusions of grandeur; "And the world passeth away" (v.17). It is all destined for the flames (2 Pet 3.10-13). But even before that momentous climax, palatial homes become ruins, swanky cars become rusty wrecks, and flamboyant styles become dated. What is the point of loving the world when it is so obviously transient? It is far better to be among those who "do the will of God" and abide for ever. When the world system is finally laid to rest, a body of people will still be in the enjoyment of things that are lasting and eternal. Do we love the world or do we do the will of God?

When providing a final evidence of the new birth in the life John says this; "whatsoever is born of God overcometh the world: and this is the victory that overcometh the world, even our faith" (1 Jn 5.4). He is demonstrating that victory over the subtlety and assaults of the world is the hallmark of everyone whose faith is genuine. A person who is permanently swamped by the world, and is constantly ensnared by the world may be regarded as a worldly Christian. The fact of the matter is that they might be just a worldly person who has known nothing of the regenerating power of the Holy Spirit!

CHAPTER 5

OLD TESTAMENT PICTURES OF THE WORLD

We have already noted that Old Testament conflicts illustrate the believer's perpetual engagement with his spiritual foes, The World, The Flesh and The Devil. We do have Scriptural authority for extracting spiritual lessons from Old Testament history; "whatsoever things were written aforetime were written for our learning" (Rom 15.4), so we turn back to the Old Testament briefly to observe that some of its locations illustrate different aspects of the world system.

Sodom

It does not take much imagination to see in Sodom a picture of the world in its immoral perverted character. The sight of two strangers in town inflamed its homosexuals to the extent that they planned a gang rape (Gen 19). A message that had been divulged to Abraham had been a scathing denunciation of such brutal disgusting behaviour. "The cry of Sodom and Gomorrah is great...their sin very grievous" (ch18.20). James Strong suggests that the word "cry" could be as intense as "shriek". It indicates the effect of the cruel vices of the men of Sodom upon their victims. If the intended gang rape was a feature of city life and not just an isolated event, it is little wonder that shrieks of terror were constantly ascending to heaven.

If you were able to ignore the huge level of sexual perversion with its attendant violence, life in Sodom was progressing very satisfactorily. The Lord Jesus gave an insight into the seeming normality of the social life of the city; "they did eat, they drank". There was a buzz about what people would now call "the high street"; "they bought, they sold". The agriculture industry and the construction industry were both healthy; "they planted, they builded" (Lk 17.28). But behind that façade of seeming normality there was a cesspool of moral corruption, depravities that were no longer practised in the closet but paraded brazenly, and condoned and even promoted by the general public. It is a mirror image of life in many localities today.

In the Western world, there are still many who are repulsed by the race to push back the boundaries of what were once regarded as the respectable norms of morality. Others hypocritically spout what is expected of them in condemning bad behaviour and are then exposed as offenders themselves! However, it is clear from the increasing stories of child abuse and misbehaviour on the part of public figures that what is reported may be just the tip of a very unhealthy iceberg that has had a chilling moral effect on society at large. Believers should be intolerant of the world of Sodom in its various manifestations. The danger is that we can become so inured to what is prevalent that we lose the awareness of just how repugnant it is to our God. We really need to have our moral compass well set.

Egypt

Egypt was the place where the people of Israel had been held in slavery before their redemption. It too provides a valid picture of the world system that bound us before the emancipating experience of conversion. In particular, it illustrates the pleasures that the world provides, for connected with Egypt are "the pleasures of sin" (Heb 11.25). Significantly, we are told that for Moses these pleasures would have been "for a season", an indication of the transient nature of any of the enjoyments of the world. Even a hardened sinner like Robert Burns was honest enough to acknowledge how short-lived worldly amusements are. In his epic poem *Tam o' Shanter* he expressed it like this.

> But pleasures are like poppies spread,
> You seize the flow'r, its bloom is shed;
> Or like the snow falls in the river,
> A moment white - then melts for ever;
> Or like the Borealis race, (Scots for rays!)
> That flit ere you can point their place;

Or like the rainbow's lovely form
Evanishing amid the storm.

Again, these trifling pleasures are illustrated in the fact that in all the wretchedness and torture of their slavery, the Israelites had little titbits that left them with an illusion that their load had been somewhat lightened (Num 11.5). It is a sad fact that fleeting entertainments can be a huge distraction for people who are contemplating the need for salvation. The "pleasures of this life" rank with "cares and riches" as thorns that choke the good seed of the Word and impair its effectiveness (Lk 8.14). When these activities are so obviously harmful, why would any believer say as did the ancient Israelites, "Let us return into Egypt" (Num 14.4)?

Christians profess that Christ has both saved and satisfied them. "He satisfieth the longing soul" (Ps 107.9). They are "abundantly satisfied" and they "drink of the river of thy pleasure" (Ps 36.8). We sing at our meetings, "Now none but Christ can satisfy". These sentiments are denied when we frequent the places where unsaved people are questing for excitement or are in search of amusement. The truth of separation involves a geographical separation at times, that is, avoiding places where our presence would be inappropriate if we are taking into account Bible warnings about our appetite for the things of the world. Abraham's sortie into Egypt was disastrous (Gen 12.9-20). Isaac was warned, "Go not down into Egypt" (Gen 26.2). A solitary visit to a stadium or a theatre could start a trend that leads to spiritual collapse. Why risk the danger?

Jericho

Jericho seems to present a more appealing side of the world than the seedy pop culture, or the uncompromising rivalry of competitive sport that erupts so easily into violence. It is described as "the city of palm trees" (Deut 34.3). Its citizens reckoned that "the situation of this city is pleasant", but they had to acknowledge that "the water is naught, and the ground barren" (2 Kings 2.19). In other words, although the environment was so appealing, the land around was totally unproductive.

Doubtless there is a side to the world that is sophisticated, cultural and classical. It appears to be innocent, but it is "barren" as far as the child of God is concerned. It contributes nothing to his spiritual life, gives him no increased appreciation of his Saviour, and robs him of time that could be used more profitably in the service of God. For the child of God, the "works of darkness" are "unfruitful" (Eph 5.11). The world of Jericho does nothing to enrich the believer's life.

Babylon

Babylon (Babel) is first mentioned in the Bible in connection with Nimrod, and as well as his expansionist ambitions, the events surrounding Babel are indicative of his attempts to create a rival religion involving the worship of heavenly bodies (Gen 10.8-10; 11.1-9). Babylon was the cradle of idolatry and right through to the final book of the Bible, Babylon is seen as a sinister religious system in bitter opposition to the genuine people of God (Rev 17).

In the early centuries of Christianity there was fierce persecution, first at the hands of the Jews and then from the Roman Empire. Constantine reversed that trend, but when he popularised the Christian religion, he absorbed into it many of the old pagan features. That, plus the incorporation of Old Testament rituals, rendered Christianity almost unrecognisable, a system far removed from primitive New Testament conditions. The marriage of church and state was disastrous and even the momentous work of the Reformation has not eliminated that sad legacy. The Babylonish system with its worldly religion is still alive and well.

There are many genuine believers who have stepped back from that system and are content to be connected to congregations with a desire to replicate New Testament principles and to allow them to govern their mode of gathering. The paraphernalia of religion has no place in their activities and they follow a simple form of worship and service that holds no appeal for the unregenerate or carnal mind. They recognise Babylon for what it is, another manifestation of the world though in a religious guise.

Enemy number one, The World; let us be alert to the danger it poses, and avoid it in its various shapes and forms for inevitably, it will cripple us spiritually.

CHAPTER 6

THE FLESH

A Definition

The word "flesh" is another of those Bible words whose meaning must be determined by its context. On occasions it is a simple reference to the bodies of men or beasts. For example, "All flesh is not the same flesh" (1 Cor 15.39); all Paul was saying is that on earth there are different kinds of bodies, for God has created all His creatures with a body suited to the environment in which they function, fish in water and so on. Speaking about his own life-span Paul referred to himself living "in the flesh" (Phil 1.22) and "the life which I now live in the flesh" (Gal 2.20). The Lord's term on earth is described as "the days of his flesh" (Heb 5.7). The phrase obviously relates to His presence in this world in a body.

Sometimes the word carries the concept of mankind. For example, when speaking of the horrific conditions of the Great Tribulation, the Lord Jesus indicated that the earth's population will be savagely reduced, so that "except those days should be shortened, there should no flesh be saved" (Mt 24.22), that is, mankind would become extinct. Paul used the word in that way when he said, "by the deeds of the law there shall no flesh be justified in his sight" (Rom 3.20). That is, none of mankind will ever be justified by law-keeping.

Obviously, neither of these usages fits the bill as far as the study of our enemies is concerned. It is clear that when the Bible uses the term in that connection it relates to **our sinful nature**. That is not a Bible expression, but the tenor of Scripture sits comfortably with the idea of The Flesh being our old sinful nature. W.E. Vine described it as "the seat of sin in the believer". Scripture describes the flesh as "*sinful* flesh" (Rom 8.3) and "*filth*" is connected with it (1 Pet 3.21).

It might be appropriate at this juncture to indicate that "the flesh" and "the old man" are not synonymous terms. We shall notice that the flesh is still with us; it has never been removed. However, at conversion we "put off the old man with his deeds; and have put on the new man" (Col 3.9-10). "The old man" is what we were in unconverted days as people connected to Adam, and at conversion that old life style with its "deeds" was abandoned. In God's reckoning it was dealt with at the cross when our old man was "crucified with him, that the body of sin might be destroyed", that is, rendered idle (Rom 6.6). So from God's standpoint, the fact that we have been linked with Christ in His crucifixion has dealt with our old man; in practice, we were severed from him at conversion and in repentance we repudiated his "deeds". Please note though that the flesh was not put off at conversion, and it remains as a huge annoyance and a constant threat to our spiritual lives.

"They that are in The Flesh".

The Bible defines unsaved people as "they that are in the flesh" (Rom 8.8), and such people "cannot please God". In other words, the unregenerate have never begun to please God no matter how moral or religious they are. Everyone born into this world has inherited the fallen sinful nature; it has been passed on from Adam right through every generation. When Adam fathered Seth, he did so "in his own likeness, after his image" (Gen 5.3). By that time he was a fallen sinful creature so his sinful nature was being transmitted to the next generation and right down through. "That which is born of the flesh is flesh" (Jn 3.6), and hence the need for the new birth. We did not require regeneration because of anything that we had ever done. Forgiveness was essential for the sins that we had committed, but the new birth was necessary just because of what we were by nature.

The sinful nature is incorrigible, totally hostile to God and completely insubordinate; in fact its character is such that under no circumstances would it ever acknowledge God's authority. "The carnal mind (the mind of the flesh) is enmity against God: for it is not subject to the law of God, *neither indeed can be*" (Rom 8.7). So then, in light of the fact that the sinful nature is so intractable even God made no attempt to improve it. The new birth imparts to the believing man or woman the divine nature (2 Pet

1.4); at that point the Holy Spirit entered, so that we are now described as being "not in the flesh, but in the Spirit" (Rom 8.9).

Tension

The fact that the flesh has neither been removed nor improved at conversion means that the believer's life is now a battle ground and that tensions exist that were never there before; "fleshly lusts...war against the soul" (1 Pet 2.11). There is a traitor within us who is undermining us and is so happy to collaborate with our external foes. "The lust of the flesh" is mentioned in connection with our enemy the world (1 Jn 2.16). James refers to our "own lust" when raising the issue of temptation, and the tempter is our enemy the devil (1 Thess 3.5), so the enticement to evil finds a willing collaborator within us who ten times out of ten would jump at the opportunity to sin (James 1.14). "I know that in me (that is, in my flesh,) dwelleth no good thing" (Rom 7.18). Our lives are war-zones where the enemy within the gate is constantly hampering spiritual aspirations. This whole scenario can create unhappiness and frustration and the "O wretched man that I am!" is wrung from many a heart (Rom 7.24).

Power for Victory

Quelling the activity of the flesh is not down to will power and self-effort. Determination to keep the law of God is not the answer either, for Romans ch.7 shows that just as law-keeping played no part in our justification (Rom

3.20,28), so it plays no part in our sanctification, that is, our ability to lead a holy life. In our union with Christ we have died to the law, "that we should serve in newness of spirit, and not in the oldness of the letter" (Rom 7.6). The power for Christian living lies in the Holy Spirit Who dwells within us.

God's law made demands on us but gave no power to perform; it was "weak through the flesh" (Rom 8.3), but in sending His Son, God triggered events that would lead to people walking "after the Spirit" and being thus equipped to fulfil "the righteousness of the law" (v.4). It is "through the Spirit" that we can put to death "the deeds of the body" (v.13). Thus there is constant need to realise our dependence on Him and to co-operate with Him in our lives.

Our Responsibility

The awareness of our absolute dependence on the Spirit of God should never leave us complacent and in a state of inertia. We do have a responsibility to be active in countering the activity of the flesh in our lives. Paul gives genuine believers credit for having dealt with the flesh; "they that are Christ's have crucified the flesh with the affections and lusts" (Gal 5.24). There is an ongoing need to "put ye on the Lord Jesus Christ, and make not provision for the flesh, to fulfil the lusts thereof" (Rom 13.14). Putting on the Lord Jesus means cultivating the character of Christ in our own lives, reproducing His moral qualities. That will never happen if we are catering for the flesh. The things that we read, watch and focus on can all enflame the flesh and distort the mirror image of the Saviour that ought to be in evidence in each of us. To get down to the practicalities once more, it demands the stringent control of all the gadgetry that is available to us. Going off-piste on the Internet invites an avalanche of filth that could sweep you to spiritual disaster. Even the level of distraction created by smartphones, tablets and laptops can seriously impinge on our main focus of developing our spiritual lives and being committed to the service of our Lord.

The Works of the Flesh

Galatians ch.5 speaks of the tensions that have been referred to, the flesh lusting against the Spirit and the Spirit against the flesh (v.17). Allowing the Spirit to control us, walking in the Spirit, deters us from fulfilling "the lust of the flesh" (v.16). The context underscores just how obnoxious the flesh is when Paul refers to "the works of the flesh" (v.19). There is a lengthy list of very disagreeable sins and attitudes, vulgar, violent behaviour that is the hallmark of people who will never "inherit the kingdom of God" (v.21). Be clear; persistent and perpetual commitment to "the works of the flesh" demonstrates that the perpetrators have never been saved.

In contrast to the works of the flesh, Paul speaks about "the fruit of the Spirit" (Gal 5.22). The word "works" conveys the idea of commotion; boisterous, noisy, activity. "Fruit" leaves us with the impression of the Spirit of God working quietly in our lives, promoting growth and development and this lovely cluster of fruit that is so reminiscent of the beauty of our Lord Jesus Christ. The contrast between the works of the flesh and the fruit of the Spirit is stark, so let us repudiate the one and cultivate the other as empowered by the Holy Spirit Himself.

While genuine believers will never continually display the works of the flesh, it is sadly possible for flashes of fleshly activity to come to the fore. For example, Paul charged the Corinthians with being "carnal", a word allied to "flesh". Their fleshly behaviour was demonstrated in "envying, and strife, and divisions" and was the kind of conduct that was common among the unsaved; they were walking "as men" (1 Cor 3.3). The rivalries, animosities and polarization that were a feature of Corinthian life had infiltrated the church of God at Corinth, and it was just a display of the flesh on the part of these believers. May God preserve us from allowing fleshly activity to disturb the harmony of His assembly.

The flesh is a formidable foe then, and we shall never be clear of its menacing influence until we are safe home in glory.

CHAPTER 7

AMALEK AND EGLON

As with the world, there are Old Testament illustrations of the flesh, notably Amalek, and Eglon king of Moab. It is because of their origins that we see them as portrayals of the flesh. Amalek was a grandson of Esau, a man who displayed fleshly desires to the exclusion of spiritual privileges; he preferred to satisfy his bodily needs with a plate of lentil soup than to enjoy the spiritual benefits connected with his birthright (Gen 25.29-34). Amalek's father was Eliphaz, and really he was the illegitimate son of Eliphaz's concubine (Gen 36.12), so all things considered, we feel that Amalek stands as a valid illustration of the flesh.

Eglon was king of Moab ((Judg 3.12-30). Again, the origins of Moab permit us to see in him a picture of the flesh. He was the product of an incestuous relationship between Lot and his elder daughter (Gen 19.37). Eglon himself was a man of immense proportions, "a very fat man" (Judg 3.17), and again, in putting all the data together we consider that we are justified in seeing in him a visual aid of the flesh.

Amalek

To follow the history of Amalek would take us far off track, but one incident will suffice to demonstrate the subtlety of the flesh. The people of Israel had been redeemed from the bondage of Egypt and were now en route to Canaan. The Red Sea was behind them, severing their links with their place of enslavement. A pillar of cloud, indicative of God's presence, led the way. They had begun to enjoy the manna, and had just received refreshing water from the rock (Ex 16-17); "Then came Amalek, and fought with Israel" (Ex 17.8). Amalek was unprincipled and subtle; "he smote the hindmost of thee, even all that were feeble behind thee, when thou wast faint and weary; and he feared not God" (Deut 25.18).

Israel's history finds a parallel in our spiritual experience. At conversion, we were freed from the tyranny of evil by the blood of the Lamb. We have been delivered and separated from "this present evil world" (Gal 1.4). God's Spirit and God's Word give guidance for our pilgrimage. Christ, the Bread of God, sustains our spiritual lives while we ponder Him in the Word. The refreshing ministry of the Holy Spirit quenches our spiritual thirst. "Then came Amalek". We are particularly vulnerable if we have allowed ourselves to lag behind and have permitted ourselves to become enfeebled by neglecting the spiritual nourishment of the Word. The flesh will take advantage and strike so unexpectedly.

To many who are newly saved it comes as a shock that there are still issues with the flesh. Perhaps preachers left them with the impression that after salvation they would be virtually sinless, and that life would be seamless. Maybe they were under the impression that they were now immune from many of the things that troubled them in unconverted days. "Then came Amalek!". What a shock to discover that the traitor within us is active and clamouring for VIP treatment; some fleshly desire demands indulgence. The song of deliverance (Ex 15) has hardly died on our lips when an old habit tries to reassert itself. Unbidden, an evil suggestion darts through the mind. How discouraging to find that on occasions we experience defeat, but the lesson from Exodus 17 is that victory is possible.

While the battle was being fought in the valley, Moses was interceding on the hilltop, an imperfect picture of the Lord's ministry of intercession and succour. I say "imperfect" because there is never any suggestion of fatigue and inconstancy with Him as there was with Moses. How good to know that "he is able" because "he ever liveth to make intercession for (us)" (Heb 7.25). Watching Moses, Aaron and Hur ascending the hill also reminds us that we need to be constantly interceding for each other in life's warfare.

While Moses was interceding on the hilltop, Joshua was in conflict in the wilderness, and victory was secured "with the edge of the sword" (v.13). The sword is a figure of "the word of God" (Eph 6.17), so while the Lord's activity for us is a crucial factor in our conflict, we must apply the Word to any given situation and decisively put to death any sins of the flesh (Col 3.5).

The fact that the Lord would have war with Amalek "from generation to generation" (v.16) was an indication that Israel's victory over him in their spiritual infancy did not infer that the war was over. He would be back as a constant irritation, a disrupter of their day-to-day lives, and it is just an indication of what we have already observed, that the flesh will never be removed, and will be a perpetual source of exasperation until the end of our journey here.

Eglon

On entering the promised land, the Moabites were among Israel's earliest oppressors (Judg 3.12-30). Sin had occasioned this subjugation (v.12), but after eighteen years their misery was such that God responded to their appeal for relief. Eglon was Moab's monarch, and God raised up Ehud to deal with him (v.15). As stated earlier, not only his Moabite ethnicity but also his massive proportions render him a picture of the flesh.

"Moab hath been at ease from his youth, and he hath settled on his lees" (Jer 48.11). A feature of the flesh is to indulge self, and Eglon precisely fits the bill. He was a glutton; (Judg 3.17); when others were suffering from the debilitating heat, he was cossetted in his summer parlour and such was his selfish nature that he had its exclusive use! (v.20). How self-centred the flesh is!

Ehud's two-edged sword (v.16 R.V.) dealt with him and once more we have a reminder of the Word of God that is "living, and powerful, and sharper than any two-edged sword" (Heb 4.12). Ehud had to manufacture his long dagger, an indication that there is great need for us to be familiar with the Word and to make it our own before it will be of any use to us. Reading the Bible, meditating on its message, studying its chapters will all stand us in good stead in this conflict with the flesh.

Without elaborating the gory details, Ehud knew exactly where to administer the fatal stab (v.21). It is for us to identify our personal flaws, to discover what the Scriptures have to say about that particular area of failure, and then "through the Spirit" to "mortify the deeds of the body" (Rom 8.13). If so, "ye shall live", the spiritual answer to the land having "rest" after the conquest of Eglon and his hosts (v.30). Once again though, our illustration serves notice that the war with the flesh will never end this side of the glory, for Scripture tells us that "Moab was subdued", but certainly not annihilated!

O hide this self from me that I
No more, but Christ in me may live!
My vile affections mortify,
Nor let one darling sin survive:
In all things nothing may I see,
Nothing desire, or seek, but Thee.
        (Gerhard Tersteegen).

CHAPTER 8

THE DEVIL; HIS ORIGINS AND DOOM

Origins

A verse in the last book of the Bible indicates that in our third foe there combines a cocktail of very unpleasant characteristics, cruelty, subtlety, duplicity and hostility (Rev 20.2). He is "the dragon", his cruelty. He is "that old serpent", his subtlety. He is "the Devil", meaning a slanderer, his duplicity. He is Satan, meaning an adversary, his hostility. Without even pulling in descriptions from elsewhere, there is sufficient in that word picture to depict an enemy with immense resources and with the tremendous potential to do us damage. It is little wonder that when Peter speaks about the devil's designs upon us, he urges us to be extremely alert; "Be sober, be vigilant" (1 Pet 5.8).

There are two passages of Scripture that give a clue to his origins. It has to be acknowledged that not every Bible teacher sees him depicted in these verses, but most do. He is portrayed as the king of Babylon and the king of Tyre (Is 14.3-23; Ezek 28.11-19). Taking these passages together, it is evident that originally he was one of the cherubim, perhaps the most senior of all God's angels. His wisdom and beauty were unique, but these attributes created pride and a spirit of insubordination that erupted in outright rebellion, an attempt to oust God! His watchword was, "I will be like the most High". It seems that many angels came under his influence and supported the mutiny so that the Lord Jesus spoke of "the devil and his angels" (Mt 25.41), and John referred to "the dragon…and his angels" (Rev 12.7). Again, Bible teachers are divided on this, but it is possible that there was a subsequent defection of angels, those who are described by Peter as "the angels that sinned" (2 Pet 2.4) and by Jude as "the angels which kept not their first estate" (Jude 6). That particular group has been "cast… down to hell" (2 Pet 2.4), while it appears that like Satan, angels involved in the original rebellion have freedom of movement and are the demons who feature so extensively in the Gospels.

First Encounter

The Scriptures have hardly begun when we have our first encounter with this malignant being. Immediately we are alerted to his power, for he commandeered a serpent, gave it the ability to communicate, and used it to deceive Eve, a fact that is mentioned in two New Testament contexts (Gen 3; 2 Cor 11.3; 1 Tim 2.14). No doubt he was irked at God vesting in Adam such supreme authority over His creation (Ps 8.6-8), and so he targeted the man, using his wife as the means of inciting him to disobey God. Of course, his attack was the product of his ongoing loathing of a holy God, and one of his attempts to thwart any plan that God may set in motion.

Right at the start he used tactics that feature throughout his career. Subtlety was key to his strategy rather than the less effective stormy aggression that he sometimes employs. He waited till Eve was alone before he approached her. He then cast doubt on what God had said; "Hath God said?" (Gen 3.1). He advanced to blatantly contradicting what God had said; "Ye shall not surely die" (v.4). Then he insinuated that God was depriving them (v.5). The Lord Jesus said, "he is a liar, and the father of lies" (Jn 8.44 ESV). That blend of casting doubt, lying and insinuation was sufficient to ensnare Eve, and so his first attack on humanity was a resounding success. It would be 4000 years before he tasted defeat when in his encounter with the Son of God in the wilderness he at last faced a holy man Who would never respond to his seductions!

His Doom

"Whosoever shall exalt himself shall be abased (humbled)" (Mt 23.12). The Lord's words are supremely exemplified in the experience of Satan. The first downward step was his expulsion from heaven, "fallen from heaven" (Is 14.12). What was once his environment was no longer his permanent abode, although it does appear that on occasions

God summons him to give account of his movements (Job 1.6-7; 2.1-2). He is presently described as "the prince of the power of the air" (Eph 2.2) so he operates freely in the atmosphere around the planet, and indeed can set up headquarters on the earth itself. In late apostolic times his centre of operations was the city of Pergamos (Rev 2.13); he was domiciled there, his throne was there, the nerve centre of his activities was there. It would be speculative to suggest where his seat of operations is today though with different dubious credentials, many locations are competing for the doubtful honour!

The next downward step for Satan will be at the mid-point of the Tribulation period, a seven year period of time that will commence subsequent to the rapture of the church. There will be "war in heaven" with the protagonists an army of angels under the command of Michael and an army of demons directed by "the dragon" (Rev 12.7-12). A vanquished Satan will be "cast out into the earth", to be confined there for the remainder of the Tribulation. Knowing his limited time, his fury will know no bounds, his malevolence adding to the wrath of God to make these three and a half years "great tribulation", (Mt 24.21). No wonder the Scriptures say, "Woe to the inhabiters of the earth" (Rev 12.12).

In particular, during his confinement to earth he will make the nation of Israel the focus of his spite, which is one of the reasons for that period being called, "the time of Jacob's trouble" (Jer 30.7). However, God will preserve the nation from total annihilation; "he shall be saved out of it", and the record of God's miraculous intervention is in the latter part of Revelation 12.

During that era, a man controlled and empowered by the devil will stride the world stage. The Bible calls him "The Beast". The dragon will give this man his power, his throne and his authority (Rev 13.2), but the beast and his allies will be routed when the Lord Jesus returns in power and glory, and he and the false prophet will be cast alive into the lake of fire (Rev 19.19-21). At the same point the devil will be arrested and bound, and cast into the bottomless pit for the thousand years of Christ's reign over the earth (Rev 20.1-3).

At the end of the thousand years, he will be released briefly, long enough to foment the last rebellion against divine authority. Multitudes who will be born during the kingdom era will harbour resentment against the strict moral and ethical code of the theocratic regime. Open hostility would invite swift retribution from Him Who will rule with a rod of iron, but a secret dislike of the King will be there. The devil will find in such hearts fertile soil for the seeds of revolt, but that last insurgency will be quashed instantly, and at that point the devil will be taken and assigned to his final and eternal place of imprisonment, the lake of fire (Rev 20.7-10). The language employed is horrifying; with the beast and the false prophet he will be "tormented day and night for ever and ever".

So then, it is downhill all the way for the evil one; heaven, the air, earth, the bottomless pit, the lake of fire. Exalting himself, he will certainly be abased, but take no comfort from that, for presently he is still active, and we must perceive him to be a constant threat to our spiritual progress, our effective service, and our enjoyment of Christ.

Satan's downward spiral was settled by the work of the Lord Jesus at the cross. Through His death, the Saviour would "destroy ('bring to naught' RV; 'annul' JND) him that had the power of death, that is, the devil" (Heb 2.14). One of the purposes for the Lord appearing in this world was to "destroy the works of the devil", His death being the event that would provide liberty for people under the domination of Satan, allowing them to quit the practice of sin, and to become the habitual exponents of righteousness (1 Jn 3.7-9). The cross is perceived as a great battleground where the Lord Jesus sent the hosts of evil into ignominious retreat and carried off the spoils of battle (Col 2.15). This victory at Calvary was the subject of the very first Bible prophecy when God intimated that the woman's Seed would crush the head of the serpent and in the process have His own heel bruised (Gen 3.15).

CHAPTER 9

SOME TITLES
OF THE DEVIL

We have already noted that a range of descriptions depict different aspects of the devil's malevolent character, each of them conspiring together to warrant John frequently describing him as "the wicked one" (e.g. 1 Jn 2.14); he is consummately evil. However, he has other designations, some of which deserve comment.

Satan

This is his most common name. It is of Hebrew origin, and denotes an opponent or adversary. Primarily, he is an opponent of God. In a parable, one of the characters is described as "an enemy", and in interpreting the parable the Lord Jesus said, "The enemy...is the devil" (Mt 13.28,39). Thus everything connected with God attracts his unwanted attention. He eyed God's throne, he spoiled God's creation, he attacked God's Son, he hates God's people and he has designs on God's assembly.

He is also an adversary of mankind in general. The Lord Jesus spoke of him binding people (Lk 13.16), and part of Paul's mission was to turn people from "the power of Satan unto God" (Acts 26.18). His great ambition is to keep the general populace in the misery of slavery and he has to his range of "achievements" the fact that he is "the deceiver of the whole world" (Rev 12.9 RV). He deceives some with atheism and others with religion. He deceives some with hedonism and others with smug self-righteousness. He deceives some with the politics of capitalism and others with the politics of communism. He deceives some with philosophical arguments and others with laidback thoughtlessness. His ingenuity knows no bounds as he effectively corrals the world's population on the broad road leading to destruction; he is their adversary.

He opposes the people of God; he did it in both Old and New Testament times. In one of Zechariah's visions, the prophet saw "Joshua the high priest standing before the angel of the Lord, and Satan standing at his right hand to resist him" ("to be his adversary" RV) (Zech 3.1). Joshua's "filthy garments" may have given the adversary legitimate cause for criticism and ammunition to vilify him, but one lesson that leaps from the page is that wherever the adversary is lurking, God is ready for action. No sooner are we told about the presence of Satan than Scripture quickly adds, "And the Lord said unto Satan, The Lord rebuke thee, O Satan" (v.2). "If God be for us, who can be against us?" (Rom 8.31). Would the One Who gave His own Son for us leave us unprotected from the adversary? Never!

In the New Testament, Paul experienced the activity of the adversary. By an undisclosed means, he blocked his return to Thessalonica, and reflecting on it, the apostle simply said, "Satan hindered us" (1 Thess 2.18). It appears too that Satan assigned a demon to monitor Paul, " a messenger of Satan" to buffet him (2 Cor 12.7-9). Paul learned to live with that, and saw it as part of God's permissive will to keep him humble. Again though, in the face of the activity of the adversary there was the assurance of divine interest and the grace that was sufficient for the trial. The attention of the adversary, whatever it was, served to give an appearance of weakness on Paul's part, but he revelled in the fact that his weakness allowed the power of Christ to rest upon him; it gave opportunity for divine power to flow out unimpeded by any pretentious attitudes or acts on the part of the servant. Satan always oversteps himself!

The Devil

This particular description indicates that he is a slanderer. When applied to people, the word is translated "false accuser" or "slanderer", particularly in the pastoral epistles. It is confirmation of the Lord's comment that "he is a liar" (Jn 8.44). Incessantly he accuses the Lord's people before God (Rev 12.10). It is well that "the blood of the Lamb" deals with the whole situation, for even though some of his accusations may be legitimate, the precious blood of Christ has dealt with these issues.

His *modus operandi* is laid bare in his dealings with Job. Intruding into an angelic conference he was challenged about Job's integrity and piety. His immediate reaction was to question Job's motives and predict his renunciation of God should his favourable circumstances change (Job 1.6-12). He is the devil, a slanderer, a false accuser.

Getting down to practicalities, he employs human agencies to vilify God's people, as when Potiphar's wife blatantly libelled Joseph (Gen 39.7-23). It took years for him to be cleared, and in the meantime there was the stigma, as the whiff of scandal hung around him, and there was the suffering as the iron entered his soul. The cruelty of the devil is boundless, as he does all in his power to discredit the people of God.

His slanderous conduct is seen extensively in his dealings with the Lord Jesus. For example, in a context where the Lord told the people that they were "of (their) father the devil", they gave evidence of it by their scurrilous remark, "Say we not well that thou art a Samaritan, and hast a devil" (Jn 8.44,48). Like father, like son! That is just a sample of the insulting defamatory remarks that the arch-slanderer made about our beloved Lord.

The Prince of This World.

An earlier chapter has drawn attention to this title, applied to Satan by the Lord Jesus (Jn 12.31). There is no need to cover the ground again, but just to remind you that he controls the world's population, dictates its trends and styles, promotes its idols of sport and entertainment, and accords its politicians power and cult status. He is dominant, the unseen manipulator of both big business and the labour movements. He is the spiritual power behind governments; we observe this in the book of Daniel where spirit beings who are designated "the prince of Persia" and "the prince of Grecia" are very evidently lieutenants of the devil who have been assigned to manipulate the affairs of these nations (Dan 10.20). So he is the unseen attendee at cabinet meetings, setting the agenda, steering the debate and swaying the decisions that are made. The influence of Satan is universally pervasive; he is the prince of this world.

The Prince of the Power of the Air.

Reference has already been made to the chapter where this title appears (Eph 2.2). It leaves us with the distinct impression that the devil is at the apex of a hierarchy of evil spirits, the angels that he had led in the initial revolt against God. When God created angels, he had placed them in ranks, described as "principality, and power, and might, and dominion" (Eph 1.21); in ascension the Lord Jesus had passed through their serried ranks to the very pinnacle of glory, "far above all". It appears that the fallen angels retained their former status, though now subject to their new leader, their prince. In Scripture they are designated by these former grades, though now the words "darkness" and "wickedness" are linked to them to demonstrate how evil their character and activity now is (Eph 6.12).

The Gospels record the activities of these beings, frequently describing them as "evil" or "unclean". There is more said about them during the Lord's presence on earth than at any other time in Bible history. It leaves the feeling that when He was resident in Israel during "the days of his flesh", Satan marshalled his forces in opposition to His activities there. It is also a sad reflection on the spiritual condition of the nation that there was so much demonic activity among the people.

These powerful spirits had the ability to possess people; they had a craving to be in some way embodied in either man or beast (Mk 5.12-13). The outcome of demon possession was varied. Some people were afflicted by physical disabilities, and some were mentally disturbed to the extent of self-harm or even the tendency to be suicidal. The superior power of Christ in expelling these malignant beings is underscored in one of His parables. He depicts Himself as One with the ability to bind the strong man (Satan), and spoil his goods (Mt 12.29). There were many who experienced the emancipating power of Christ, and one of them, Mary Magdalene, who had been enslaved by seven demons, proved to be one of His most loyal followers (Lk 8.2).

The Gentile world was not exempt from the attentions of these evil beings, and it is clear that they took advantage when people embraced idolatry in preference to the living and true God. While Paul acknowledged that "an idol is nothing" (1 Cor 8.4), he did make clear that behind the idol there was demonic activity, and in sacrificing to idols men were sacrificing to demons (1 Cor 10.14-22). Their subservience to demons explains the seemingly miraculous things that are an integral part of idolatrous ceremonies. In some lands, what would seem to be dangerous and harmful rituals that would normally maim or kill are carried through without blood being shed and without a bruise or a scar being left. As early as Exodus 7, the Bible shows that satanic power can replicate at least some of God's activities as when the magicians of Egypt duplicated the early plagues. It is worthwhile remembering that the miraculous is not always evidence of God at work!

Reference has been made to the lands where idolatry with its attendant demonic activity is still prevalent. That is not to infer that western society is a no-go area for these servants of the devil. Undoubtedly their influence is increasing and we need to be aware of that. However, in some areas of evangelicalism there is the danger of seeing evil spirits around every corner, when in fact rampant evil can be the product of wicked human hearts, and physical infirmities and mental health issues are the price of being part of the groaning creation that is the product of the fall (Rom 8.19-25).

It is against these foot soldiers of the devil that we are in constant conflict (Eph 6.10-20). The Bible depicts us wrestling with them; it is a constant hand-to-hand encounter that necessitates us "taking the whole armour of God". Truth, righteousness, peace and faith are all seen as essential parts of our equipment. The enjoyment of salvation will protect our minds, and the application of the sword of the Spirit (the Word of God) to any situation will repel the attack. Should the assault come from longer range and the fiery arrows of doubt come raining in, the shield of faith gives adequate cover.

Please note that the armour has to "taken"; it will do us no good if we refuse to wear it. The cunning character of the foe is again stressed when Paul speaks of "the wiles of the devil" (v.11). He has never subscribed to the Geneva Convention; for him it is a "no holds barred" policy with recourse to dirty tricks; hence the need for the whole armour. Paul speaks about "the evil day" (v.13), the day of stress for you, the day of satanic attack, the day when you are the target. The whole armour has to be taken in order to "withstand" on that day of intense pressure so that when the smoke of battle has cleared you are still standing (v.13), and are able to say, "I thank God through Jesus Christ our Lord" (Rom 7.25).

Praying and "watching" are crucial if we are to be alert to the possibility of a surprise attack (v.18). In the very first war, the victorious kings had never anticipated a surprise nocturnal reprisal and it was their downfall (Gen 14.15). The people of Laish "dwelt careless...quiet and secure"; they were an easy prey for the warriors of the tribe of Dan (Judg 18.7; 27-29). Syria's Ben-hadad had a laidback attitude to Ahab's attack (1 Kings 20.12-21); it resulted in a resounding defeat. These military tales from Bible days serve to illustrate the danger of complacency for the Christian soldier. "Be strong"; "put on the whole armour"; "stand"; "pray"; "watch"; each of these injunctions in Ephesians 6 encourages vigilance and the need to constantly scan the horizon for signs of spiritual danger.

Before moving on from this topic of Satan's underlings, it may be worth noting that from earliest days mankind has had a fascination for their spiritual activities; that inquisitive attitude persists until this present time. Many people have a deep interest in the occult, witchcraft, séances, Ouija boards and the like. In Isaiah's day rather than seeking God, the people encouraged each other to "Seek unto them that have familiar spirits, and unto wizards that peep (chirp), and that mutter" (Is 8.19). That was in flagrant defiance of God. In His law He had forbidden any contact with mediums, (Lev 19.31), and had declared it a capital offence (ch.20.27). The crowning sin of King Saul was to consult such a person and he was dead by the next day (1 Sam 28). Never allow even curiosity to encourage you to familiarise yourself with the workings of spiritualism and the occult. It is true that there are many charlatans with an eye for profit connected to these activities, but that should never mask the fact that behind it all there is demonic power and activity; give it a wide berth at all times.

The God of This World

On only one occasion, the devil is described as "the god of this world (age)" (2 Cor 4.4), and the title indicates that he not only is the world's prince, dictating its trends and dominating its people, but also its god, demanding its worship. The Bible speaks of a time in the future when men shall knowingly and willingly worship the dragon (Rev 13.4), but even now, many are unconsciously religiously loyal to him. The fact that they do not believe "the glorious gospel of Christ, who is the image of God" means that their hearts are charmed by other things, and in idolising and prioritising these other things they are avowing their allegiance to Satan rather than to God, and thus he is the god of this age.

His business is to keep the gospel "hid", that is, "veiled" to those who do not believe, and he has achieved this in expert fashion by "blinding (their) minds". I have suggested earlier some ways in which he has gone about his underhand activity to keep people in the dark but 2 Corinthians 4 has particular reference to the gospel. He will tell some that they do not require it; they are good enough the way they are. Some will see it as foolishness that a man on a cross was accomplishing a work whereby sinners could be saved and forgiven. Others will baulk at the idea of faith alone being the pathway to blessing; it surely requires a major contribution from them! So by adding to the gospel, and by twisting the gospel and by diluting the gospel, one way or another the "god of this world" retains his devotees.

CHAPTER 10

SATAN'S PRESENT ACTIVITY

His Activity in the World

We have just been noting that part of the devil's business in the world is to blind the minds of unbelievers. It was shown previously that he enslaves the men of the world; they are under his power (Acts 26.18). He "oppresses" them, oftentimes through demonic activity (Acts 10.38). However, in the "kingdom parables" of Matthew 13, two other interesting but frightening facts emerge. First, he has the ability to snatch away the seed of the Word of God. In the parable of the sower, seed that fell on the hard-packed pathway was soon food for the birds (Mt 13.4). In giving the interpretation, the Lord Jesus indicated that people who do not grasp the message when it is preached are immediately targeted by the devil, and he "snatcheth away that which hath been sown in his heart" (v.19 RV). It is staggering to think that he has the ability to remove things from the minds of men and women. Perhaps he uses distractions to divert them from giving further thought to something that they have found difficult to grasp, but by some means or another, he achieves his end.

Not only does he have the ability to extract things from people's minds, but he can also implant thoughts in their hearts. It was Satan who put it into the heart of Judas Iscariot to betray the Lord (Jn 13.2), and in that case, he then possessed Judas to personally superintend the act of betrayal (v.27). This was one task that he did not delegate to any of his underling principalities or powers; it was too important, but the initial step was to put the thought into Judas's mind.

He also incited Ananias to act out a lie when disposing of his property. Peter indicated that it was Satan who filled his heart "to lie to the Holy Ghost" (Acts 5.3). No wonder the Bible tells us; "Keep thy heart with all diligence; for out of it are the issues of life" (Prov 4.23). So, the evil one can remove helpful thoughts from the mind and he can insert harmful thoughts into the mind; his power and subtlety know no bounds.

Another of the parables tells of an enemy sowing tares among wheat (Mt 13.25). Once more, the Lord Himself gave the interpretation. In this parable, the "good seed" represents "the children of the kingdom", genuine believers in the Lord Jesus Christ. The tares represent, "the children of the wicked one", sown by "the enemy", "the devil" (vv. 36-43). The warning is that in the field (the world,) growing side by side there are true believers and those who claim to be Christians but have never been born again. Initially, they may resemble the children of God, but then they display the features of "(their) father the devil" (Jn 8.44). Inevitably, the children of God and the children of the devil are "manifested", that is, the family to which a person belongs becomes evident by their behaviour (1 Jn 3.10). Elymas demonstrated that he was "a child of the devil" because he was "full of all subtilty and all mischief" and was an "enemy of all righteousness" (Acts 13.10).

The facts of the parable are borne out in the world of Christendom where multitudes bear the name "Christian" but have known nothing of God's saving grace in their lives. Tares come in a religious guise; not all the "children of the evil one" belong to the criminal fraternity or espouse an atheistic viewpoint. Many of them would be outraged if you questioned their claim to be "Christian", and yet the devil's great aim is to keep people content with the outward show of religion and ritual without the basic experience of regeneration. What they have is an inoculation against the real thing.

It should be stressed that while the Lord taught the inevitability of religious profession, he was not suggesting that wheat and tares should coexist in a New Testament assembly. It is in "the field" that they grow together, and He explained that "the field is the world" (Mt 13.38). While it was and is possible for assemblies to be infiltrated, the norm is that they comprise of a total believing membership; they are "churches *of the saints*" (1 Cor 14.33). That is the Scriptural position rather than the mixed membership that is normal and acceptable in many of the congregations of Christendom.

His Activity in the Assembly.

New Testament assemblies were the focus of satanic interest in a number of ways. For example, the assembly at Corinth was in danger of being infiltrated by men from a Jewish background who were trying to undermine Paul and his teaching; Paul branded them Satan's "ministers" (2 Cor 11.15), and that whole chapter is devoted to his denunciation of them and his defence of his own position as an apostle of Christ. Their tactics were characteristic of their mentor, beguiling with subtlety in the same fashion as the serpent had deceived Eve (v.3), and masquerading as "ministers of righteousness" in the same way as the devil tries to pass himself as "an angel of light" (v.14).

The lesson is that by devious means, the devil will try to corrupt and distort clear Bible teaching by using very plausible men to penetrate the assembly. Their manner may be courteous and their character may be personable, but they are satanic plants who with very suave and convincing oratory can sway assembly members against the truth of God. We all need to be aware of their underhand activity, and overseers in particular must be as vigilant as the Ephesian elders were encouraged to be when Paul warned them of "grievous wolves" who would "enter in among you, not sparing the flock" (Acts 20.29). If the devil is successful in promoting false teaching, it destroys the "chaste virgin" aspect of the assembly, that is, the fact that it is a place where wholesome, unadulterated, God-given scriptural doctrine should be taught and believed and practised.

Another of Satan's ploys is to keep an unforgiving spirit simmering among assembly members (2 Cor 2.5-11). Paul calls it one of the evil one's "devices", and indicates that if successful, he is getting "the advantage" over us. At Corinth they were slow to forgive an erring member who had truly repented, but as a general principle, to allow an unforgiving spirit to linger destroys fellowship, and permanent resentments severely hamper any possibility of "striving together for the faith of the gospel" (Phil 1.27). So then, he endeavours to corrupt doctrine, and he attempts to fracture relationships, any one of which could be to the destruction of assembly testimony.

One further resource in his armoury is to discredit assembly elders, and so he endeavours to ensnare them (1 Tim 3.7). His work is made easy if the elder or potential elder makes no effort to maintain a healthy reputation among outsiders. If bad behaviour destroys his testimony then he has invited "reproach" and has in fact blundered into a satanic trap that disqualifies him from functioning as an elder. A strategy to take out the leadership is a master plan, so the shepherds in any assembly need to be particularly on their guard; for them to be discredited is a massive coup for the devil, and has far-reaching ramifications for the assembly as a whole.

His Activity in the Lives of Individual Believers

A number of Scriptures throw light on the devil's designs on each believer and his tactics to bring them down. On the eve of His death, the Lord Jesus spoke to Simon Peter of Satan's desire to sift him and his fellow-disciples as wheat (Lk 22.31). Normally a sifting process is to remove the chaff. Undoubtedly the devil's idea was to remove the wheat! So he put these men in the sieve and all the commotion and agitation and shaking to and fro that they would experience would allow him to remove the wheat! He wanted to throw them into a set of disturbing circumstances in an attempt to destroy their faith. Anticipating this severe satanic onslaught, the Lord said specifically to Peter, "I have prayed for thee, that thy faith fail not" (v.32). In the intense sifting process Peter's courage failed him, but in answer to the Lord's intercession, his faith never failed! He experienced recovery and subsequently in his life he was used in a remarkable way.

No doubt the evil one still has similar designs on the people of God. As with Job, he uses distracting circumstances to disturb, and all the tossing and shaking in the "sieve" is calculated to unsettle them spiritually, to dent their faith, and to send them into reverse gear as far as their commitment to God is concerned. It is so good to know that as with Simon Peter, we have an Intercessor Who prays for us. "It is Christ that died, yea rather, that is risen again, who is even at the right hand of God, *who also maketh intercession for us*" (Rom 8.34). "Wherefore he is able also to save them to the uttermost that come unto God by him, *seeing he ever liveth to make intercession for them*" (Heb 7.25). Fortified by a divine Intercessor's activity for us, we can survive the sifting process when the evil one puts in his request to have us to sift us as wheat.

At times, Satan's policy is to stir up high-level persecution against believers and Peter warned of this when he described him as a "roaring lion" prowling in search of prey (1 Pet 5.8). Peter's original readership had known much of the ferocity of persecution, with a fresh wave about to break; it was a "fiery trial" that would "try" them (ch.4.12), but he encouraged them by speaking of a God Who cared, (ch.5.7), of brethren who were in similar circumstances (v.9), and of the "eternal glory" that would be the sequel to their suffering (v.10). Other believers experienced similar vicious treatment at the hands of satanically inspired men. At Smyrna, they were "about to suffer" and the devil "was about to" cast some of them into prison (Rev 2.10 RV), and yet the word of encouragement from the Lord was this, "Be thou faithful unto death, and I will give thee a crown of life". Antipas was martyred at Pergamos, "where Satan dwelleth" (Rev 2.13).

Throughout the centuries, Satan has maintained these tactics of intimidation. God's people have been beaten or even martyred. Their property has been confiscated and many have been displaced. Threats of torture and imprisonment have hung over their heads, and many have been deprived of employment with subsequent privation. In the face of all that aggression, multitudes of loyal souls have remained true to Christ.

For many years, believers in the western world have been spared the worst excesses of persecution, but they still have to share the reproach of Christ. The abuse may be exclusively verbal, but cynical remarks, angry tirades, and blasphemous comments serve to unsettle the timid and grieve the soul. Unsaved relatives, neighbours and colleagues can put their best efforts into making life a misery for the child of God. So the devil still operates like a roaring lion but in the face of his ferocious attacks, the Christian can be like the apostles who rejoiced because "they were counted worthy to suffer shame for his name" (Acts 5.41).

Satan's roaring-lion tactics were a regular feature of the book of Acts, but in almost every situation where he stirred hatred and persecution, his policy was counter productive. For example, the extensive persecution that followed the martyrdom of Stephen resulted in refugee believers being scattered in every direction, and wherever they went they carried the message of the gospel (Acts 11.19). Without the harassment they experienced, they would hardly likely have been as quick to fan out to these other regions with the message of life. Perhaps a stalled evangelical expansion is the result of the easy-going soft-option Christianity that stems from being tolerated rather than persecuted!

Very likely, Satan's most successful strategy is to tempt believers to commit sin. Twice over in the Bible he is called "the tempter". On the first occasion it is the description that Matthew gave him as he prepared to face the Lord Jesus after the Saviour's forty-day fast in the wilderness; "The tempter came to him" (Mt 4.3). As has already been noted, for the very first time in four thousand years of human history, "the tempter" would face defeat as he used every weapon in his armoury in a futile endeavour to ensnare God the Son, Who "cannot be tempted with evil" (James 1.13).

The second usage of the word "tempter" is when Paul was writing to the Thessalonians. Because Satan had hindered him from going to Thessalonica, he had sent Timothy to minister, and then to bring him word of their spiritual condition. He was anxious "lest by some means the tempter have tempted you, and our labour be in vain" (1 Thess 3.5). Once more, the tempter's onslaught had been ineffective, for Timothy was able to return to Paul with good news of their faith and love (v.6).

It has to be said though, that temptation is a very potent manoeuvre in Satan's range of activities. When thinking about the flesh, attention was drawn to James ch. 1 where James shows that sin is the result of us being drawn away by our own lusts in response to an external enticement (v.14). Another phrase of which mention was made speaks of "the snare of the devil" (1 Tim 3.7). These Scriptures paint a picture of a baited snare calculated to entrap an unwary animal. Thus Satan sets his snares for unwary believers. He knows precisely the kind of bait that appeals to each, and thus he varies his enticements to suit the potential victim. He panders to the lazy; he incites the workaholic. He uses the nerve-tingling excitement of a sporting contest as well as the relaxing atmosphere of the cultural concert. In some, he promotes a sullen rude disposition. In others, he encourages a talkative outgoing personality that specialises in gossip that verges on the slanderous. There is the temptation to tell a lie if it will save face and embarrassment. There is the temptation to make a "fast buck" dishonestly if it can be done without detection. There are experiences that appear daring and exciting but can end in shame or addiction. In a huge variety of ways he spreads his snares and lays his bait; he is "the tempter" and it is in this role that we encounter him most.

In light of that, we stress once more the great need for vigilance. As stated previously, we wrestle against his various lieutenants, and hence the need to "put on the whole armour of God" (Eph 6.11). The Lord Jesus Himself used "the sword of the Spirit" as in the temptation He constantly quoted the Scriptures; "It is written". That same resource is available to us in the hour of temptation but it demands us being familiar with the Word, so that it can be applied suitably and skilfully in any given situation. A variety of New Testament writers encourage resilience. Paul; "neither give place to the devil" (Eph 4.27). James; "Resist the devil, and he will flee from you" (James 4.7). Peter; "whom resist stedfast in the faith" (1 Pet 5.9). John; "overcome the wicked one" (1 Jn 2.13). Taken together, we have the picture of a daunting foe, but one who can be challenged and conquered in the power of the indwelling Holy Spirit. May God help us all to be "more than conquerors through him that loved us" (Rom 8.37).

Conclusion.

Three enemies, The World, The Flesh and The Devil; each of them in its own way is determined to undermine the believer's spiritual life, dampen his commitment to God, and ruin his effectiveness in service. To go back to where we started, with divine help let us like Caleb withstand our three foes and expel them from Hebron so that our fellowship with God will be sweet and uninterrupted. Let us like Benaiah who figured in David's honours list overcome our three enemies so that we may feature in Christ's honours list when He expresses His "well done" at the Judgment Seat.

MORE BOOKS
BY JACK HAY

A Mini Commentary on 1st John

The first in our new Pocket Commentary Series by Ritchie Publications offering short outlines on various books of the Bible at affordable prices. Jack Hay's commentary on 1st John represents articles that were originally written for a series included in the Believer's Magazine. An excellent outline on the book of 1st John and the handy size allows it to be easily stored and given to young people who may not normally sit down with a larger sized commentary.

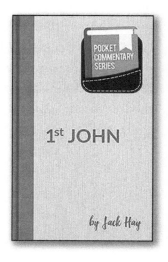

9781910513682

Abraham
Character Study Series

This is the second book in the Ritchie Character Study Series. Recognising the benefit that comes from a study of Bible characters, the publishers have commissioned a series of such studies. This volume has been written by well-known evangelist and Bible teacher Jack Hay.

9781910513774

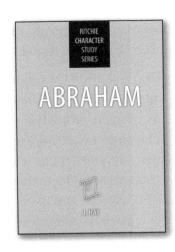

An Introduction to Bible Prophecy

People have always been intrigued with the future. In Bible days, the trappings of the occult featured in Nebuchadnezzar's quest for guidance (Ezek 21.21), and soothsaying was alive and well in ancient Philippi (Acts 16.16).

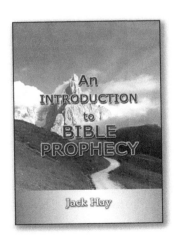

That fascination has not diminished with the onset of a secular scientific age. The trend lives on, and today, horoscopes, ouija boards, seances and fortune-telling all play a significant part in modern society.

Believers are satisfied that the only safe source of information about the future is the inspired Word Of God.

The goal of this booklet is to provide an introduction to the subject of Bible prophecy. The approach will be elementary, keeping in mind the young believer or the new believer who may be exploring these truths for the first time. For many readers then, it will be merely a refresher course, a restatement of facts they have known for many years, but it is hoped that it will be helpful to "stir up your pure minds by way of remembrance" (2 Pet 3.1).

9781907731532

Baptism

This booklet sets out in simple terms what the Bible teaches about Christian baptism. The major part of the presentation is intended to be a help to people who have begun to take an interest in the Scriptures, or who have perhaps recently become Christians. It explains from the New Testament 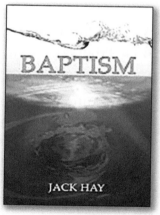 that one of the next steps on the pathway of faith is baptism. For believers who have been on the Christian road a little longer, appendices have been added to deal with some of the more complex aspects of the subject.

9781904064978

Safe, Sure and Happy

The Bible teaches clearly that there is life after death.

One day each of us will reach the end of life here and move out into eternity, but eternity where?

The aim of this booklet is to explain, from the Bible,

- how you can be safe in heaven for eternity

- how you can be sure you are forgiven

- how you can have a happy life on the way to heaven.

9781907731983

The Holy Spirit

This short book about the Holy Spirit has been written to help young believers in Christ to understand what the Bible teaches about this important subject. We are informed from the Scriptures about who the Holy Spirit is and what He does. Like other books and booklets

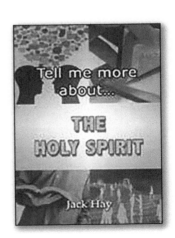

in this series, the style of writing has been kept simple. It will therefore be easier to read, and also to translate into other languages where this is necessary or helpful. The end of chapter summaries and optional study questions will help all readers absorb the subject matter and take their studies further.

9781907731594